Mark
tells the good news

A quick look at this book

KT-162-128

CHAPTER 1

John the Baptist Prepares the Way

Here begins the Good News about Jesus the Messiah, the Son of God.[1]

In the book of the prophet Isaiah, God said,

"Look, I am sending my messenger before you,
and he will prepare your way.[2]
He is a voice shouting in the wilderness:
'Prepare a pathway for the Lord's coming!
Make a straight road for him!'[3]"

This messenger was John the Baptist. He lived in the wilderness and was preaching that people should be baptized to show that they had turned from their sins and turned to God to be forgiven.[4]

People from Jerusalem and from all over Judea travelled out into the wilderness to see and hear John. And when they confessed their sins, he baptized them in the River Jordan. His clothes were woven from camel hair, and he wore a leather belt; his food was locusts and wild honey. He announced: "Someone is coming soon who is far greater than I am — so much greater that I am not even worthy to be his slave.[5] I baptize you with[6] water, but he will baptize you with the Holy Spirit!"

The Baptism of Jesus

One day Jesus came from Nazareth in Galilee, and he was baptized by John in the River Jordan. And when Jesus came up out of the water, he saw the heavens split open and the Holy Spirit descending like a dove on him. And a voice came from heaven saying, "You are my beloved Son, and I am fully pleased with you."

The Temptation of Jesus

Immediately the Holy Spirit compelled Jesus to go into the wilderness. He was there for forty days, being tempted by Satan. He was out among the wild animals, and angels took care of him.

The First Disciples

Later on, after John was arrested by Herod Antipas, Jesus went to Galilee to preach God's Good News. "At last the time has come!" he announced. "The Kingdom of God is near! Turn from your sins and believe this Good News!"

One day as Jesus was walking along the shores of the Sea of Galilee, he saw Simon[7] and his brother, Andrew, fishing with a net, for they were commercial fishermen. Jesus called out to them, "Come, be my disciples, and I will show you how to fish for people!" And they left their nets at once and went with him.

A little farther up the shore Jesus saw Zebedee's sons, James and John, in a boat mending their nets. He called them, too, and immediately they left their father, Zebedee, in the boat with the hired men and went with him.

Jesus Casts Out an Evil Spirit

Jesus and his companions went to the town of Capernaum, and every Sabbath day he went into the synagogue and taught the people. They were amazed at his teaching, for he taught as one who had real authority — quite unlike the teachers of religious law.

A man possessed by an evil spirit was in the synagogue, and he began shouting, "Why are you bothering us, Jesus of Nazareth? Have you come to destroy us? I know who you are — the Holy One sent from God!"

Jesus cut him short. "Be silent! Come out of the man." At that, the evil spirit screamed and threw the man into a convulsion, but then he left him.

Amazement gripped the audience, and they began to discuss what had happened. "What sort of new teaching is this?" they asked excitedly. "It has such authority! Even evil spirits obey his orders!" The news of what he had done spread quickly through that entire area of Galilee.

Jesus Heals Many People

After Jesus and his disciples left the synagogue, they went over to Simon and Andrew's home, and James and John were with them. Simon's mother-in-law was sick in bed with a high fever. They told Jesus about her right away. He went to her bedside, and as he took her by the hand and helped her to sit up, the fever suddenly left, and she got up and prepared a meal for them.

That evening at sunset, many sick and demon-possessed people were brought to Jesus. And a huge crowd of people from all over Capernaum gathered outside the door to watch. So Jesus healed great numbers of sick people who had many different kinds of diseases, and he ordered many demons to come out of their victims. But because they knew who he was, he refused to allow the demons to speak.

Jesus Preaches in Galilee

The next morning Jesus awoke long before daybreak and went out alone into the wilderness to pray. Later, Simon and the others went out to find him. They said, "Everyone is asking for you."

But he replied, "We must go on to other towns as well, and I will preach to them, too, because that is why I came." So he travelled throughout the region of Galilee, preaching in the synagogues and expelling demons from many people.

Jesus Heals a Man with Leprosy

A man with leprosy came and knelt in front of Jesus, begging to be healed. "If you want to, you can make me well again," he said.

Moved with pity,[8] Jesus touched him. "I want to," he said. "Be healed!" Instantly the leprosy disappeared — the man was healed. Then Jesus sent him on his way and told him sternly, "Go right over to the priest and let him examine you. Don't talk to anyone along the way. Take along the offering required in the law of Moses for those who have been healed of leprosy, so everyone will have proof of your healing."

But as the man went on his way, he spread the news, telling everyone what had happened to him. As a result, such crowds soon surrounded Jesus that he couldn't enter a town anywhere publicly. He had to stay out in the secluded places, and people from everywhere came to him there.

CHAPTER 2

Jesus Heals a Paralysed Man

Several days later Jesus returned to Capernaum, and the news of his arrival spread quickly through the town. Soon the house where he was staying was so packed with visitors that there wasn't room for one more person, not even outside the door. And he preached the word to them. Four men arrived carrying a paralysed man on a mat. They couldn't get to Jesus through the crowd, so they dug through the clay roof above his head. Then they lowered the sick man on his mat, right down in front of Jesus. Seeing their faith, Jesus said to the paralysed man, "My child, your sins are forgiven."

But some of the teachers of religious law who were sitting there said to themselves, "What? This is blasphemy! Who but God can forgive sins!"

Jesus knew what they were discussing among themselves, so he said to them, "Why do you think this is blasphemy? Is it easier to say to the paralysed man, 'Your sins are forgiven' or 'Get up, pick up your mat, and walk'? I will prove that I, the Son of Man, have the authority on earth to forgive sins." Then Jesus turned to the paralysed man and said, "Stand up, take your mat, and go on home, because you are healed!"

The man jumped up, took the mat, and pushed his way through the stunned onlookers. Then they all praised God. "We've never seen anything like this before!" they exclaimed.

Jesus Calls Levi (Matthew)

Then Jesus went out to the lakeshore again and taught the crowds that gathered around him. As he walked along, he saw Levi, son of Alphaeus, sitting at his tax-collection booth. "Come, be my disciple," Jesus said to him. So Levi got up and followed him.

That night Levi invited Jesus and his disciples to be his dinner guests, along with his fellow tax collectors and many other notorious sinners. (There were many people of this kind among the crowds that followed Jesus.) But when some of the teachers of religious law who were Pharisees[1] saw him eating with people like that, they said to his disciples, "Why does he eat with such scum[2]?"

When Jesus heard this, he told them, "Healthy people don't need a doctor — sick people do. I have come to call sinners, not those who think they are already good enough."

A Discussion about Fasting

John's disciples and the Pharisees sometimes fasted. One day some people came to Jesus and asked, "Why do John's disciples and the Pharisees fast, but your disciples don't fast?"

Jesus replied, "Do wedding guests fast while celebrating with the groom? Of course not. They can't fast while they are with the groom. But some day he will be taken away from them, and then they will fast. And who would patch an old garment with unshrunk cloth? For the new patch shrinks and pulls away from the old cloth, leaving an even bigger hole than before. And no one puts new wine into old wineskins. The wine would burst the wineskins, spilling the wine and ruining the skins. New wine needs new wineskins."

A Discussion about the Sabbath

One Sabbath day as Jesus was walking through some cornfields, his disciples began breaking off heads of wheat. But the Pharisees said to Jesus, "They shouldn't be doing that! It's against the law to work by harvesting corn on the Sabbath."

But Jesus replied, "Haven't you ever read in the Scriptures what King David did when he and his companions were hungry? He went into the house of God (during the days when Abiathar was high priest), ate the special bread reserved for the priests alone, and then gave some to his companions. That was breaking the law, too." Then he said to them, "The Sabbath was made to benefit people, and not people to benefit the Sabbath. And I, the Son of Man, am master even of the Sabbath!"

CHAPTER 3

Jesus Heals on the Sabbath

Jesus went into the synagogue again and noticed a man with a deformed hand. Since it was the Sabbath, Jesus' enemies watched him closely. Would he heal the man's hand on the Sabbath? If he did, they planned to condemn him. Jesus said to the man, "Come and stand in front of everyone." Then he turned to his critics and asked, "Is it legal to do good deeds on the Sabbath, or is it a day for doing harm? Is this a day to save life or to destroy it?" But they wouldn't answer him. He looked around at them angrily, because he was deeply disturbed by their hard hearts. Then he said to the man, "Reach out your hand." The man reached out his hand, and it became normal again! At once the Pharisees went away and met up with the supporters of Herod to discuss plans for killing Jesus.

Crowds Follow Jesus

Jesus and his disciples went out to the lake, followed by a huge crowd from all over Galilee, Judea, Jerusalem, Idumea, from east of the River Jordan, and even from as far away as Tyre and Sidon. The news about his miracles had spread far and wide, and vast numbers of people came to see him for themselves.

Jesus instructed his disciples to bring around a boat and to have it ready in case he was crowded off the beach. There had been many healings that day. As a result, many sick people were crowding around him, trying to touch him. And whenever those possessed by evil spirits caught sight of him, they would fall down in front of him shrieking, "You are the Son of God!" But Jesus strictly warned them not to say who he was.

Jesus Chooses the Twelve Apostles

Afterwards Jesus went up on a mountain and called the ones he wanted to go with him. And they came to him. Then he selected twelve of them to be his regular companions, calling them apostles.[1] He sent them out to preach, and he gave them authority to cast out demons. These are the names of the twelve he chose:

Simon (he renamed him Peter),

James and John (the sons of Zebedee, but Jesus nicknamed them "Sons of Thunder"[2]),
Andrew,
Philip,
Bartholomew,
Matthew,
Thomas,
James (son of Alphaeus),
Thaddaeus,
Simon (the Zealot[3]),
Judas Iscariot (who later betrayed him).

Jesus and the Prince of Demons

When Jesus returned to the house where he was staying, the crowds began to gather again, and soon he and his disciples couldn't even find time to eat. When his family heard what was happening, they tried to take him home with them. "He's out of his mind," they said.

But the teachers of religious law who had arrived from Jerusalem said, "He's possessed by Satan,[4] the prince of demons. That's where he gets the power to cast out demons."

Jesus called them over and said to them by way of illustration, "How can Satan cast out Satan? A kingdom at war with itself will collapse. A home divided against itself is doomed. And if Satan is fighting against himself, how can he stand? He would never survive. Let me illustrate this. You can't enter a strong man's house and rob him without first tying him up. Only then can his house be robbed![5]

"I assure you that any sin can be forgiven, including blasphemy; but anyone who blasphemes against the Holy

9

Spirit will never be forgiven. It is an eternal sin." He told them this because they were saying he had an evil spirit.

The True Family of Jesus

Jesus' mother and brothers arrived at the house where he was teaching. They stood outside and sent word for him to come out and talk with them. There was a crowd around Jesus, and someone said, "Your mother and your brothers and sisters[6] are outside, asking for you."

Jesus replied, "Who is my mother? Who are my brothers?" Then he looked at those around him and said, "These are my mother and brothers. Anyone who does God's will is my brother and sister and mother."

CHAPTER 4

Story of the Farmer Scattering Seed

Once again Jesus began teaching by the lakeshore. There was such a large crowd along the shore that he got into a boat and sat down and spoke from there. He began to teach the people by telling many stories such as this one:

"Listen! A farmer went out to plant some seed. As he scattered it across his field, some seed fell on a footpath, and the birds came and ate it. Other seed fell on shallow soil with underlying rock. The plant sprang up quickly, but it soon wilted beneath the hot sun and died because the roots had no nourishment in the shallow soil. Other seed fell among thorns that shot up and choked out the tender blades so that it produced no grain. Still other seed fell on fertile soil and produced a crop that was thirty, sixty, and even a hundred times as much as had been planted." Then he said, "Anyone who is willing to hear should listen and understand!"

Later, when Jesus was alone with the twelve disciples and with the others who were gathered around, they asked him, "What do your stories mean?"

He replied, "You are permitted to understand the secret about the Kingdom of God. But I am using these stories to conceal everything about it from outsiders, so that the Scriptures might be fulfilled:

'They see what I do,
but they don't perceive its meaning.
They hear my words,
but they don't understand.
So they will not turn from their sins
and be forgiven.'[1]

"But if you can't understand this story, how will you understand all the others I am going to tell? The farmer I talked about is the one who brings God's message to others. The seed that fell on the hard path represents those who hear the message, but then Satan comes at once and takes it away from them. The rocky soil represents those who hear the message and receive it with joy. But like young plants in such soil, their roots don't go very deep. At first they get along fine, but they wilt as soon as they have problems or are persecuted because they believe the word. The thorny ground represents those who hear and accept the Good News, but all too quickly the message is crowded out by the cares of this life, the lure of wealth, and the desire for nice things, so no crop is produced. But the good soil represents those who hear and accept God's message and produce a huge harvest — thirty, sixty, or even a hundred times as much as had been planted."

Illustration of the Lamp

Then Jesus asked them, "Would anyone light a lamp and then put it under a basket or under a bed to shut out the light? Of course not! A lamp is placed on a stand, where its light will shine.

"Everything that is now hidden or secret will eventually be brought to light. Anyone who is willing to hear should listen and understand! And be sure to pay attention to what you hear. The more you do this, the more you will understand — and even more, besides. To those who are open to my teaching, more understanding will be given. But to those who are not listening, even what they have will be taken away from them."

Illustration of the Growing Seed

Jesus also said, "Here is another illustration of what the Kingdom of God is like: A farmer planted seeds in a field, and then he went on with his other activities. As the days went by, the seeds sprouted and grew without the farmer's help, because the earth produces crops on its own. First a leaf blade pushes through, then the heads of wheat are formed, and finally the grain ripens. And as soon as the grain is ready, the farmer comes and harvests it with a sickle."

Illustration of the Mustard Seed

Jesus asked, "How can I describe the Kingdom of God? What story should I use to illustrate it? It is like a tiny mustard seed. Though this is one of the smallest of seeds, it grows to become one of the largest of plants, with long branches where birds can come and find shelter."

He used many such stories and illustrations to teach the people as much as they were able to understand. In fact, in his public teaching he taught only with parables, but afterwards when he was alone with his disciples, he explained the meaning to them.

Jesus Calms the Storm

As evening came, Jesus said to his disciples, "Let's cross to the other side of the lake." He was already in the boat, so they started out, leaving the crowds behind (although other boats followed). But soon a fierce storm arose. High waves began to break into the boat until it was nearly full of water.

Jesus was sleeping at the back of the boat with his head on a cushion. Frantically they woke him up, shouting, "Teacher, don't you even care that we are going to drown?"

When he woke up, he rebuked the wind and said to the water, "Silence! Be still!" Suddenly the wind stopped, and there was a great calm. And he asked them, "Why are you so afraid? Do you still not have faith in me?"

And they were filled with awe and said among themselves, "Who is this man, that even the wind and waves obey him?"

CHAPTER 5

Jesus Heals a Demon-Possessed Man

So they arrived at the other side of the lake, in the land of the Gerasenes.[1] Just as Jesus was climbing from the boat, a man possessed by an evil spirit ran out from a cemetery to meet him. This man lived among the tombs and could not be restrained, even with a chain. Whenever he was put into chains and shackles — as he often was — he snapped the chains from his wrists and smashed the shackles. No one was strong enough to control him. All day long and throughout the night, he would wander among the tombs and in the hills, screaming and hitting himself with stones.

When Jesus was still some distance away, the man saw him. He ran to meet Jesus and fell down before him. He gave a terrible scream, shrieking, "Why are you bothering me, Jesus, Son of the Most High God? For God's sake, don't torture me!" For Jesus had already said to the spirit, "Come out of the man, you evil spirit."

Then Jesus asked, "What is your name?"

And the spirit replied, "Legion, because there are many of us here inside this man." Then the spirits begged him again and again not to send them to some distant place. There happened to be a large herd of pigs feeding on the hillside nearby. "Send us into those pigs," the evil spirits begged. Jesus gave them permission. So the evil spirits came out of the man and entered the pigs, and the entire herd of two thousand pigs plunged down the steep hillside into the lake, where they drowned.

The herdsmen fled to the nearby city and the surrounding countryside, spreading the news as they ran. Everyone rushed out to see for themselves. A crowd soon gathered around Jesus, but they were frightened when they saw the man who had been demon possessed, for he was sitting there fully clothed and perfectly sane. Those who had seen what happened to the man and to the pigs told everyone about it, and the crowd began pleading with Jesus to go away and leave them alone.

When Jesus got back into the boat, the man who had been demon possessed begged to go, too. But Jesus said, "No, go home to your friends, and tell them what wonderful things the Lord has done for you and how merciful he has been." So the man started off to visit the Ten Towns[2] of that region and began to tell everyone about the great things Jesus had done for him; and everyone was amazed at what he told them.

Jesus Heals in Response to Faith
When Jesus went back across to the other side of the lake, a large crowd gathered around him on the shore. A leader of the local synagogue, whose name was Jairus, came and fell down before him, pleading with him to heal his little daughter. "She is about to die," he said in desperation. "Please come and place your hands on her; heal her so she can live."

Jesus went with him, and the crowd thronged behind. And there was a woman in the crowd who had had a haemorrhage for twelve years. She had suffered a great deal from many doctors through the years and had spent everything she had to pay them, but she had got no better. In fact, she was worse. She had heard about Jesus, so she came up behind him through the crowd and touched the fringe of his robe. For she thought to herself, "If I can just touch his clothing, I will be healed." Immediately the bleeding stopped, and she could feel that she had been healed!

Jesus realized at once that healing power had gone out from him, so he turned round in the crowd and asked, "Who touched my clothes?"

His disciples said to him, "All this crowd is pressing around you. How can you ask, 'Who touched me?'"

But he kept on looking around to see who had done it. Then the frightened woman, trembling at the realization of what had happened to her, came and fell at his feet and told him what she had done. And he said to her, "Daughter, your faith has made you well. Go in peace. You have been healed."

While he was still speaking to her, messengers arrived from Jairus's home with the message, "Your daughter is dead. There's no use troubling the Teacher now."

But Jesus ignored their comments and said to Jairus, "Don't be afraid. Just trust me." Then Jesus stopped the crowd and wouldn't let anyone go with him except Peter and James and John. When they came to the home of the synagogue leader, Jesus saw the commotion and the weeping and wailing. He went inside and spoke to the people. "Why all this weeping and commotion?" he asked. "The child isn't dead; she is only asleep."

The crowd laughed at him, but he told them all to go outside. Then he took the girl's father and mother and his three disciples into the room where the girl was lying. Holding her hand, he said to her, "Get up, little girl!"[3] And the girl, who was twelve years old, immediately stood up and walked around! Her parents were absolutely overwhelmed. Jesus commanded them not to tell anyone what had happened, and he told them to give her something to eat.

CHAPTER 6

Jesus Rejected at Nazareth

Jesus left that part of the country and returned with his disciples to Nazareth, his home town. The next Sabbath he began teaching in the synagogue, and many who heard him were astonished. They asked, "Where did he get all his wisdom and the power to perform such miracles? He's just the carpenter, the son of Mary and brother of James, Joseph,[1] Judas, and Simon. And his sisters live right here among us." They were deeply offended and refused to believe in him.

Then Jesus told them, "A prophet is honoured everywhere except in his own home town and among his relatives and his own family." And because of their unbelief, he couldn't do any mighty miracles among them except to place his hands on a few sick people and heal them. And he was amazed at their unbelief.

Jesus Sends Out the Twelve Apostles

Then Jesus went out from village to village, teaching. And he called his twelve disciples together and sent them out two by two, with authority to cast out evil spirits. He told them to take nothing with them except a walking stick — no food, no traveller's bag, no money.

He told them to wear sandals but not to take even an extra coat. "When you enter each village, be a guest in only one home," he said. "And if a village won't welcome you or listen to you, shake off its dust from your feet as you leave. It is a sign that you have abandoned that village to its fate."

So the disciples went out, telling all they met to turn from their sins. And they cast out many demons and healed many sick people, anointing them with olive oil.

The Death of John the Baptist

Herod Antipas, the king, soon heard about Jesus, because people everywhere were talking about him. Some were saying,[2] "This must be John the Baptist come back to life again. That is why he can do such miracles." Others thought Jesus was the ancient prophet Elijah. Still others thought he was a prophet like the other great prophets of the past. When Herod heard about Jesus, he said, "John, the man I beheaded, has come back from the dead." For Herod had sent soldiers to arrest and imprison John as a favour to Herodias. She had been his brother Philip's wife, but Herod had married her. John kept telling Herod, "It is illegal for you to marry your brother's wife." Herodias was enraged and wanted John killed in revenge, but without Herod's approval she was powerless. And Herod respected John, knowing that he was a good and holy man, so he kept him under his protection. Herod was disturbed whenever he talked with John, but even so, he liked to listen to him.

Herodias's chance finally came. It was Herod's birthday, and he gave a party for his palace aides, army officers, and the leading citizens of Galilee. Then his daughter, also

18

named Herodias,[3] came in and performed a dance that greatly pleased them all. "Ask me for anything you like," the king said to the girl, "and I will give it to you." Then he promised, "I will give you whatever you ask, up to half of my kingdom!"

She went out and asked her mother, "What should I ask for?"

Her mother told her, "Ask for John the Baptist's head!"

So the girl hurried back to the king and told him, "I want the head of John the Baptist, right now, on a tray!"

Then the king was very sorry, but he was embarrassed to break his oath in front of his guests. So he sent an executioner to the prison to cut off John's head and bring it to him. The soldier beheaded John in the prison, brought his head on a tray, and gave it to the girl, who took it to her mother. When John's disciples heard what had happened, they came for his body and buried it in a tomb.

Jesus Feeds Five Thousand

The apostles returned to Jesus from their ministry tour and told him all they had done and what they had taught. Then Jesus said, "Let's get away from the crowds for a while and rest." There were so many people coming and going that Jesus and his apostles didn't even have time to eat. They left by boat for a quieter spot. But many people saw them leaving, and people from many towns ran ahead along the shore and met them as they landed. A vast crowd was there as he stepped from the boat, and he had compassion on them because they were like sheep without a shepherd. So he taught them many things.

Late in the afternoon his disciples came to him and said, "This is a desolate place, and it is getting late. Send the

crowds away so they can go to the nearby farms and
villages and buy themselves some food."

But Jesus said, "You feed them."

"With what?" they asked. "It would take a small fortune[4]
to buy food for all this crowd!"

"How much food do you have?" he asked. "Go and find
out."

They came back and reported, "We have five loaves of
bread and two fish." Then Jesus told the crowd to sit down
in groups on the green grass. So they sat in groups of fifty
or a hundred.

Jesus took the five loaves and two fish, looked up
towards heaven, and asked God's blessing on the food.
Breaking the loaves into pieces, he kept giving the bread
and fish to the disciples to give to the people. They all ate
as much as they wanted, and they picked up twelve baskets
of leftover bread and fish. Five thousand men had eaten
from those five loaves!

Jesus Walks on Water

Immediately after this, Jesus made his disciples get back
into the boat and head out across the lake to Bethsaida,
while he sent the people home. Afterwards he went up into
the hills by himself to pray.

During the night, the disciples were in their boat out in
the middle of the lake, and Jesus was alone on land. He
saw that they were in serious trouble, rowing hard and
struggling against the wind and waves. About three o'clock
in the morning[5] he came to them, walking on the water. He
started to go past them, but when they saw him walking on
the water, they screamed in terror, thinking he was a ghost.
They were all terrified when they saw him. But Jesus spoke

to them at once. "It's all right," he said. "I am here! Don't be afraid." Then he climbed into the boat, and the wind stopped. They were astonished at what they saw. They still didn't understand the significance of the miracle of the multiplied loaves, for their hearts were hard and they did not believe.

When they arrived at Gennesaret on the other side of the lake, they anchored the boat and climbed out. The people standing there recognized him at once, and they ran throughout the whole area and began carrying sick people to him on mats. Wherever he went — in villages and cities and out on the farms — they laid the sick in the market-places and streets. The sick begged him to let them at least touch the fringe of his robe, and all who touched it were healed.

CHAPTER 7

Jesus Teaches about Inner Purity
One day some Pharisees and teachers of religious law arrived from Jerusalem to confront Jesus. They noticed that some of Jesus' disciples failed to follow the usual Jewish ritual of hand washing before eating. (The Jews, especially the Pharisees, do not eat until they have poured water over their cupped hands,[1] as required by their ancient traditions. Similarly, they eat nothing bought from the market unless they have immersed their hands in water. This is but one of many traditions they have clung to — such as their ceremony of washing cups, pitchers, and kettles.[2]) So the Pharisees and teachers of religious law asked him, "Why

don't your disciples follow our age-old customs? For they eat without first performing the hand-washing ceremony."

Jesus replied, "You hypocrites! Isaiah was prophesying about you when he said,

'These people honour me with their lips,
but their hearts are far away.
Their worship is a farce,
for they replace God's commands with their own man-made teachings.'[3]

For you ignore God's specific laws and substitute your own traditions."

Then he said, "You reject God's laws in order to hold on to your own traditions. For instance, Moses gave you this law from God: 'Honour your father and mother', and 'Anyone who speaks evil of father or mother must be put to death'.[4] But you say it is all right for people to say to their parents, 'Sorry, I can't help you. For I have vowed to give to God what I could have given to you.'[5] You let them disregard their needy parents. As such, you break the law of God in order to protect your own tradition. And this is only one example. There are many, many others."

Then Jesus called to the crowd to come and hear. "All of you listen," he said, "and try to understand. You are not defiled by what you eat; you are defiled by what you say and do![6]"

Then Jesus went into a house to get away from the crowds, and his disciples asked him what he meant by the statement he had made. "Don't you understand either?" he asked. "Can't you see that what you eat won't defile you? Food doesn't come in contact with your heart, but only passes through the stomach and then comes out again." (By saying this, he showed that every kind of food is acceptable.)

22

And then he added, "It is the thought-life that defiles you. For from within, out of a person's heart, come evil thoughts, sexual immorality, theft, murder, adultery, greed, wickedness, deceit, eagerness for lustful pleasure, envy, slander, pride and foolishness. All these vile things come from within; they are what defile you and make you unacceptable to God."

The Faith of a Gentile Woman

Then Jesus left Galilee and went north to the region of Tyre.[7] He tried to keep it secret that he was there, but he couldn't. As usual, the news of his arrival spread fast. Right away a woman came to him whose little girl was possessed by an evil spirit. She had heard about Jesus, and now she came and fell at his feet. She begged him to release her child from the demon's control.

Since she was a Gentile, born in Syrian Phoenicia, Jesus told her, "First I should help my own family, the Jews.[8] It isn't right to take food from the children and throw it to the dogs."

She replied, "That's true, Lord, but even the dogs under the table are given some crumbs from the children's plates."

"Good answer!" he said. "And because you have answered so well, I have healed your daughter." And when she arrived home, her little girl was lying quietly in bed, and the demon was gone.

Jesus Heals a Deaf and Mute Man

Jesus left Tyre and went to Sidon, then back to the Sea of Galilee and the region of the Ten Towns.[9] A deaf man with a speech impediment was brought to him, and the people begged Jesus to lay his hands on the man to heal him.

23

Jesus led him to a private place away from the crowd. He put his fingers into the man's ears. Then, spitting onto his own fingers, he touched the man's tongue with the spittle. And looking up to heaven, he sighed and commanded, "Be opened!"[10] Instantly the man could hear perfectly and speak plainly!

Jesus told the crowd not to tell anyone, but the more he told them not to, the more they spread the news, for they were completely amazed. Again and again they said, "Everything he does is wonderful. He even heals those who are deaf and mute."

CHAPTER 8

Jesus Feeds Four Thousand

About this time another great crowd had gathered, and the people ran out of food again. Jesus called his disciples and told them, "I feel sorry for these people. They have been here with me for three days, and they have nothing left to eat. And if I send them home without feeding them, they will faint along the road. For some of them have come a long distance."

"How are we supposed to find enough food for them here in the wilderness?" his disciples asked.

"How many loaves of bread do you have?" he asked.

"Seven," they replied. So Jesus told all the people to sit down on the ground. Then he took the seven loaves, thanked God for them, broke them into pieces and gave them to his disciples, who distributed the bread to the crowd. A few small fish were found, too, so Jesus also blessed these and told the disciples to pass them out.

They ate until they were full, and when the scraps were picked up, there were seven large baskets of food left over! There were about four thousand people in the crowd that day, and he sent them home after they had eaten. Immediately after this, he got into a boat with his disciples and crossed over to the region of Dalmanutha.

Pharisees Demand a Miraculous Sign

When the Pharisees heard that Jesus had arrived, they came to argue with him. Testing him to see if he was from God, they demanded, "Give us a miraculous sign from heaven to prove yourself."

When he heard this, he sighed deeply and said, "Why do you people keep demanding a miraculous sign? I assure you, I will not give this generation any such sign." So he got back into the boat and left them, and he crossed to the other side of the lake.

Yeast of the Pharisees and Herod

But the disciples discovered they had forgotten to bring any food, so there was only one loaf of bread with them in the boat. As they were crossing the lake, Jesus warned them, "Beware of the yeast of the Pharisees and of Herod."

They decided he was saying this because they hadn't brought any bread. Jesus knew what they were thinking, so he said, "Why are you so worried about having no food? Won't you ever learn or understand? Are your hearts too hard to take it in? 'You have eyes — can't you see? You have ears — can't you hear?'[1] Don't you remember anything at all? What about the five thousand men I fed with five loaves of bread? How many baskets of leftovers did you pick up afterwards?"

"Twelve," they said.

"And when I fed the four thousand with seven loaves, how many large baskets of leftovers did you pick up?"

"Seven," they said.

"Don't you understand even yet?" he asked them.

Jesus Heals a Blind Man

When they arrived at Bethsaida, some people brought a blind man to Jesus, and they begged him to touch and heal the man. Jesus took the blind man by the hand and led him out of the village. Then, spitting on the man's eyes, he laid his hands on him and asked, "Can you see anything now?"

The man looked around. "Yes," he said, "I see people, but I can't see them very clearly. They look like trees walking around."

Then Jesus placed his hands over the man's eyes again. As the man stared intently, his sight was completely restored, and he could see everything clearly. Jesus sent him home, saying, "Don't go back into the village on your way home."

Peter's Declaration about Jesus

Jesus and his disciples left Galilee and went up to the villages of Caesarea Philippi. As they were walking along, he asked them, "Who do people say I am?"

"Well," they replied, "some say John the Baptist, some say Elijah, and others say you are one of the other prophets."

Then Jesus asked, "Who do you say I am?"

Peter replied, "You are the Messiah." But Jesus warned them not to tell anyone about him.

Jesus Predicts His Death

Then Jesus began to tell them that he, the Son of Man, would suffer many terrible things and be rejected by the leaders, the leading priests, and the teachers of religious law. He would be killed, and three days later he would rise again. As he talked about this openly with his disciples, Peter took him aside and told him he shouldn't say things like that.[2]

Jesus turned and looked at his disciples and then said to Peter very sternly, "Get away from me, Satan! You are seeing things merely from a human point of view, not from God's."

Then he called his disciples and the crowds to come over and listen. "If any of you wants to be my follower," he told them, "you must put aside your selfish ambition, shoulder your cross, and follow me. If you try to keep your life for yourself, you will lose it. But if you give up your life for my sake and for the sake of the Good News, you will find true life. And how do you benefit if you gain the whole world but lose your own soul[3] in the process? Is anything worth more than your soul? If a person is ashamed of me and my message in these adulterous and sinful days, I, the Son of Man, will be ashamed of that person when I return in the glory of my Father with the holy angels."

CHAPTER 9

Jesus went on to say, "I assure you that some of you standing here right now will not die before you see the Kingdom of God arrive in great power!"

The Transfiguration

Six days later Jesus took Peter, James and John to the top of a mountain. No one else was there. As the men watched, Jesus' appearance changed, and his clothing became dazzling white, far whiter than any earthly process could ever make it. Then Elijah and Moses appeared and began talking with Jesus.

"Teacher, this is wonderful!" Peter exclaimed. "We will make three shrines[1] — one for you, one for Moses and one for Elijah." He didn't really know what to say, for they were all terribly afraid.

Then a cloud came over them, and a voice from the cloud said, "This is my beloved Son. Listen to him." Suddenly they looked around, and Moses and Elijah were gone, and only Jesus was with them. As they descended the mountainside, he told them not to tell anyone what they had seen until he, the Son of Man, had risen from the dead. So they kept it to themselves, but they often asked each other what he meant by "rising from the dead".

Now they began asking him, "Why do the teachers of religious law insist that Elijah must return before the Messiah comes?"

Jesus responded, "Elijah is indeed coming first to set everything in order. Why then is it written in the Scriptures that the Son of Man must suffer and be treated with utter contempt? But I tell you, Elijah has already come, and he was badly mistreated, just as the Scriptures predicted."

Jesus Heals a Boy Possessed by an Evil Spirit

At the foot of the mountain they found a great crowd surrounding the other disciples, as some teachers of religious law were arguing with them. The crowd watched

Jesus in awe as he came towards them, and then they ran to greet him. "What is all this arguing about?" he asked.

One of the men in the crowd spoke up and said, "Teacher, I brought my son for you to heal him. He can't speak because he is possessed by an evil spirit that won't let him talk. And whenever this evil spirit seizes him, it throws him violently to the ground and makes him foam at the mouth and grind his teeth and become rigid.[2] So I asked your disciples to cast out the evil spirit, but they couldn't do it."

Jesus said to them, "You faithless people! How long must I be with you until you believe? How long must I put up with you? Bring the boy to me." So they brought the boy. But when the evil spirit saw Jesus, it threw the child into a violent convulsion, and he fell to the ground, writhing and foaming at the mouth. "How long has this been happening?" Jesus asked the boy's father.

He replied, "Since he was very small. The evil spirit often makes him fall into the fire or into water, trying to kill him. Have mercy on us and help us. Do something if you can."

"What do you mean, 'If I can'?" Jesus asked. "Anything is possible if a person believes."

The father instantly replied, "I do believe, but help me not to doubt!"

When Jesus saw that the crowd of onlookers was growing, he rebuked the evil spirit. "Spirit of deafness and muteness," he said, "I command you to come out of this child and never enter him again!" Then the spirit screamed and threw the boy into another violent convulsion and left him. The boy lay there motionless, and he appeared to be dead. A murmur ran through the crowd, "He's dead." But Jesus took him by the hand and helped him to his feet, and he stood up.

Afterwards, when Jesus was alone in the house with his disciples, they asked him, "Why couldn't we cast out that evil spirit?"

Jesus replied, "This kind can be cast out only by prayer.[3]"

Jesus Again Predicts His Death

Leaving that region, they travelled through Galilee. Jesus tried to avoid all publicity in order to spend more time with his disciples and teach them. He said to them, "The Son of Man is going to be betrayed. He will be killed, but three days later he will rise from the dead." But they didn't understand what he was saying, and they were afraid to ask him what he meant.

The Greatest in the Kingdom

After they arrived at Capernaum, Jesus and his disciples settled in the house where they would be staying. Jesus asked them, "What were you discussing out on the road?" But they didn't answer, because they had been arguing about which of them was the greatest. He sat down and called the twelve disciples over to him. Then he said, "Anyone who wants to be the first must take the last place and be the servant of everyone else."

Then he put a little child among them. Taking the child in his arms, he said to them, "Anyone who welcomes a little child like this on my behalf welcomes me, and anyone who welcomes me welcomes my Father who sent me."

Using the Name of Jesus

John said to Jesus, "Teacher, we saw a man using your name to cast out demons, but we told him to stop because he isn't one of our group."

"Don't stop him!" Jesus said. "No one who performs miracles in my name will soon be able to speak evil of me. Anyone who is not against us is for us. If anyone gives you even a cup of water because you belong to the Messiah, I assure you, that person will be rewarded.

"But if anyone causes one of these little ones who trusts in me to lose faith, it would be better for that person to be thrown into the sea with a large millstone tied around the neck. If your hand causes you to sin, cut it off. It is better to enter heaven[4] with only one hand than to go into the unquenchable fires of hell with two hands.[5] If your foot causes you to sin, cut it off. It is better to enter heaven with only one foot than to be thrown into hell with two feet.[6] And if your eye causes you to sin, gouge it out. It is better to enter the Kingdom of God half blind than to have two eyes and be thrown into hell, 'where the worm never dies and the fire never goes out'.[7]

"For everyone will be purified with fire.[8] Salt is good for seasoning. But if it loses its flavour, how do you make it salty again? You must have the qualities of salt among yourselves and live in peace with each other."

CHAPTER 10

Discussion about Divorce and Marriage

Then Jesus left Capernaum and went southward to the region of Judea and into the area east of the River Jordan. As always there were the crowds, and as usual he taught them.

Some Pharisees came and tried to trap him with this question: "Should a man be allowed to divorce his wife?"

"What did Moses say about divorce?" Jesus asked them.

"Well, he permitted it," they replied. "He said a man merely has to write his wife an official letter of divorce and send her away."[1]

But Jesus responded, "He wrote those instructions only as a concession to your hard-hearted wickedness. But God's plan was seen from the beginning of creation, for 'He made them male and female'.[2] 'This explains why a man leaves his father and mother and is joined to his wife,[3] and the two are united into one.'[4] Since they are no longer two but one, let no one separate them, for God has joined them together."

Later, when he was alone with his disciples in the house, they brought up the subject again. He told them, "Whoever divorces his wife and marries someone else commits adultery against her. And if a woman divorces her husband and remarries, she commits adultery."

Jesus Blesses the Children

One day some parents brought their children to Jesus so he could touch them and bless them, but the disciples told them not to bother him. But when Jesus saw what was happening, he was very displeased with his disciples. He said to them, "Let the children come to me. Don't stop them! For the Kingdom of God belongs to such as these. I assure you, anyone who doesn't have their kind of faith will never get into the Kingdom of God." Then he took the children into his arms and placed his hands on their heads and blessed them.

The Rich Man

As he was starting out on a trip, a man came running up to Jesus, knelt down, and asked, "Good Teacher, what should I do to get eternal life?"

"Why do you call me good?" Jesus asked. "Only God is truly good. But as for your question, you know the commandments: 'Do not murder. Do not commit adultery. Do not steal. Do not testify falsely. Do not cheat. Honour your father and mother.'5"

"Teacher," the man replied, "I've obeyed all these commandments since I was a child."

Jesus felt genuine love for this man as he looked at him. "You lack only one thing," he told him. "Go and sell all you have and give the money to the poor, and you will have treasure in heaven. Then come, follow me." At this, the man's face fell, and he went sadly away because he had many possessions.

Jesus looked around and said to his disciples, "How hard it is for rich people to get into the Kingdom of God!" This amazed them. But Jesus said again, "Dear children, it is very hard6 to get into the Kingdom of God. It is easier for a camel to go through the eye of a needle than for a rich person to enter the Kingdom of God!"

The disciples were astounded. "Then who in the world can be saved?" they asked.

Jesus looked at them intently and said, "Humanly speaking, it is impossible. But not with God. Everything is possible with God."

Then Peter began to mention all that he and the other disciples had left behind. "We've given up everything to follow you," he said.

And Jesus replied, "I assure you that everyone who has

given up house or brothers or sisters or mother or father or children or property, for my sake and for the Good News, will receive now in return, a hundred times over, houses, brothers, sisters, mothers, children and property — with persecutions. And in the world to come they will have eternal life. But many who seem to be important now will be the least important then, and those who are considered least here will be the greatest then.[7]"

Jesus Again Predicts His Death

They were now on the way to Jerusalem, and Jesus was walking ahead of them. The disciples were filled with dread and the people following behind were overwhelmed with fear. Taking the twelve disciples aside, Jesus once more began to describe everything that was about to happen to him in Jerusalem. "When we get to Jerusalem," he told them, "the Son of Man will be betrayed to the leading priests and the teachers of religious law. They will sentence him to die and hand him over to the Romans. They will mock him, spit on him, beat him with their whips and kill him, but after three days he will rise again."

Jesus Teaches about Serving Others

Then James and John, the sons of Zebedee, came over and spoke to him. "Teacher," they said, "we want you to do us a favour."

"What is it?" he asked.

"In your glorious Kingdom, we want to sit in places of honour next to you," they said, "one at your right and the other at your left."

But Jesus answered, "You don't know what you are

asking! Are you able to drink from the bitter cup of sorrow I am about to drink? Are you able to be baptized with the baptism of suffering I must be baptized with?"

"Oh yes," they said, "we are able!"

And Jesus said, "You will indeed drink from my cup and be baptized with my baptism, but I have no right to say who will sit on the thrones next to mine. God has prepared those places for the ones he has chosen."

When the ten other disciples discovered what James and John had asked, they were indignant. So Jesus called them together and said, "You know that in this world kings are tyrants, and officials lord it over the people beneath them. But among you it should be quite different. Whoever wants to be a leader among you must be your servant, and whoever wants to be first must be the slave of all. For even I, the Son of Man, came here not to be served but to serve others, and to give my life as a ransom for many."

Jesus Heals Blind Bartimaeus
And so they reached Jericho. Later, as Jesus and his disciples left town, a great crowd was following. A blind beggar named Bartimaeus (son of Timaeus) was sitting beside the road as Jesus was going by. When Bartimaeus heard that Jesus from Nazareth was nearby, he began to shout out, "Jesus, Son of David, have mercy on me!"

"Be quiet!" some of the people yelled at him.

But he only shouted louder, "Son of David, have mercy on me!"

When Jesus heard him, he stopped and said, "Tell him to come here."

So they called the blind man. "Cheer up," they said.

"Come on, he's calling you!" Bartimaeus threw aside his coat, jumped up, and came to Jesus.

"What do you want me to do for you?" Jesus asked.

"Teacher," the blind man said, "I want to see!"

And Jesus said to him, "Go your way. Your faith has healed you." And instantly the blind man could see! Then he followed Jesus down the road.[8]

CHAPTER 11

The Triumphal Entry

As Jesus and his disciples approached Jerusalem, they came to the towns of Bethphage and Bethany, on the Mount of Olives. Jesus sent two of them on ahead. "Go into that village over there," he told them, "and as soon as you enter it, you will see a colt tied there that has never been ridden. Untie it and bring it here. If anyone asks what you are doing, just say, 'The Lord needs it and will return it soon.'"

The two disciples left and found the colt standing in the street, tied outside a house. As they were untying it, some bystanders demanded, "What are you doing, untying that colt?" They said what Jesus had told them to say, and they were permitted to take it. Then they brought the colt to Jesus and threw their garments over it, and he sat on it.

Many in the crowd spread their coats on the road ahead of Jesus, and others cut leafy branches in the fields and spread them along the way. He was in the centre of the procession, and the crowds all around him were shouting,

"Praise God![1]

Bless the one who comes in the name of the Lord!
Bless the coming kingdom of our ancestor David!
Praise God in highest heaven!"[2]

So Jesus came to Jerusalem and went into the Temple.
He looked around carefully at everything, and then he left
because it was late in the afternoon. Then he went out to
Bethany with the twelve disciples.

Jesus Curses the Fig Tree

The next morning as they were leaving Bethany, Jesus felt
hungry. He noticed a fig tree a little way off that was in full
leaf, so he went over to see if he could find any figs on it.
But there were only leaves because it was too early in the
season for fruit. Then Jesus said to the tree, "May no one
ever eat your fruit again!" And the disciples heard him
say it.

Jesus Clears the Temple

When they arrived back in Jerusalem, Jesus entered the
Temple and began to drive out the merchants and their
customers. He knocked over the tables of the money
changers and the stalls of those selling doves, and he
stopped everyone from bringing in merchandise. He taught
them, "The Scriptures declare, 'My Temple will be called a
place of prayer for all nations', but you have turned it into a
den of thieves."[3]

When the leading priests and teachers of religious law
heard what Jesus had done, they began planning how to
kill him. But they were afraid of him because the people
were so enthusiastic about Jesus' teaching. That evening
Jesus and the disciples[4] left the city.

The next morning as they passed by the fig tree he had

cursed, the disciples noticed it was withered from the roots. Peter remembered what Jesus had said to the tree on the previous day and exclaimed, "Look, Teacher! The fig tree you cursed has withered!"

Then Jesus said to the disciples, "Have faith in God. I assure you that you can say to this mountain, 'May God lift you up and throw you into the sea', and your command will be obeyed. All that's required is that you really believe and do not doubt in your heart. Listen to me! You can pray for anything, and if you believe, you will have it. But when you are praying, first forgive anyone against whom you are holding a grudge, so that your Father in heaven will forgive your sins, too.[5]"

The Authority of Jesus Challenged

By this time they had arrived in Jerusalem again. As Jesus was walking through the Temple area, the leading priests, the teachers of religious law and the other leaders came up to him. They demanded, "By whose authority did you drive out the merchants from the Temple?[6] Who gave you such authority?"

"I'll tell who gave me authority to do these things if you answer one question," Jesus replied. "Did John's baptism come from heaven or was it merely human? Answer me!"

They talked it over among themselves. "If we say it was from heaven, he will ask why we didn't believe him. But do we dare say it was merely human?" For they were afraid that the people would start a riot, since everyone thought that John was a prophet. So they finally replied, "We don't know."

And Jesus responded, "Then I won't answer your question either."

CHAPTER 12

Story of the Evil Farmers

Then Jesus began telling them stories: "A man planted a vineyard, built a wall around it, dug a pit for pressing out the grape juice and built a lookout tower. Then he leased the vineyard to tenant farmers and moved to another country. At grape-picking time he sent one of his servants to collect his share of the crop. But the farmers grabbed the servant, beat him up and sent him back empty-handed.

"The owner then sent another servant, but they beat him over the head and treated him shamefully. The next servant he sent was killed. Others who were sent were either beaten or killed, until there was only one left — his son whom he loved dearly. The owner finally sent him, thinking, 'Surely they will respect my son.'

"But the farmers said to one another, 'Here comes the heir to this estate. Let's kill him and get the estate for ourselves!' So they grabbed him and murdered him and threw his body out of the vineyard.

"What do you suppose the owner of the vineyard will do?" Jesus asked. "I'll tell you — he will come and kill them all and lease the vineyard to others. Didn't you ever read this in the Scriptures?

'The stone rejected by the builders
has now become the cornerstone.
This is the Lord's doing,
and it is marvellous to see.'[1]"

The Jewish leaders wanted to arrest him for using this illustration because they realized he was pointing at them — they were the wicked farmers in his story. But they were afraid to touch him because of the crowds. So they left him and went away.

Taxes for Caesar

The leaders sent some Pharisees and supporters of Herod to try to trap Jesus into saying something for which he could be arrested. "Teacher," these men said, "we know how honest you are. You are impartial and don't have favourites. You sincerely teach the ways of God. Now tell us — is it right to pay taxes to the Roman government or not? Should we pay them or should we not?"

Jesus saw through their hypocrisy and said, "Whom are you trying to fool with your trick questions? Show me a Roman coin,[2] and I'll tell you." When they handed it to him, he asked, "Whose picture and title are stamped on it?"

"Caesar's," they replied.

"Well, then," Jesus said, "give to Caesar what belongs to him. But everything that belongs to God must be given to God." This reply completely amazed them.

Discussion about Resurrection

Then Jesus was approached by some Sadducees — a group of Jews who say there is no resurrection after death. They posed this question: "Teacher, Moses gave us a law that if a man dies, leaving a wife without children, his brother should marry the widow and have a child who will be the brother's heir.[3] Well, there were seven brothers. The oldest of them married and then died without children. So the second brother married the widow, but soon he too died and left no children. Then the next brother married her and died without children. This continued until all the brothers had married her and died, and still there were no children. Last of all, the woman died, too. So tell us, whose wife will she be in the resurrection? For all seven were married to her."

Jesus replied, "Your problem is that you don't know the Scriptures, and you don't know the power of God. For when the dead rise, they won't be married. They will be like the angels in heaven. But now, as to whether the dead will be raised — haven't you ever read about this in the writings of Moses, in the story of the burning bush? Long after Abraham, Isaac and Jacob had died, God said to Moses,[4] 'I am the God of Abraham, the God of Isaac and the God of Jacob.'[5] So he is the God of the living, not the dead. You have made a serious error."

The Most Important Commandment
One of the teachers of religious law was standing there listening to the discussion. He realized that Jesus had answered well, so he asked, "Of all the commandments, which is the most important?"

Jesus replied, "The most important commandment is this: 'Hear, O Israel! The Lord our God is the one and only Lord. And you must love the Lord your God with all your heart, all your soul, all your mind and all your strength.'[6] The second is equally important: 'Love your neighbour as yourself.'[7] No other commandment is greater than these."

The teacher of religious law replied, "Well said, Teacher. You have spoken the truth by saying that there is only one God and no other. And I know it is important to love him with all my heart and all my understanding and all my strength, and to love my neighbours as myself. This is more important than to offer all of the burnt offerings and sacrifices required in the law."

Realizing this man's understanding, Jesus said to him, "You are not far from the Kingdom of God." And after that, no one dared to ask him any more questions.

Whose Son Is the Messiah?

Later, as Jesus was teaching the people in the Temple, he asked, "Why do the teachers of religious law claim that the Messiah will be the son of David? For David himself, speaking under the inspiration of the Holy Spirit, said,

'The LORD said to my Lord,

Sit in honour at my right hand

until I humble your enemies beneath your feet.'[8]

Since David himself called him Lord, how can he be his son at the same time?" And the crowd listened to him with great interest.

Here are some of the other things he taught them at this time: "Beware of these teachers of religious law! For they love to parade in flowing robes and to have everyone bow to them as they walk in the market places. And how they love the seats of honour in the synagogues and at banquets. But they shamelessly cheat widows out of their property, and then, to cover up the kind of people they really are, they make long prayers in public. Because of this, their punishment will be the greater."

The Widow's Offering

Jesus went over to the collection box in the Temple and sat and watched as the crowds dropped in their money. Many rich people put in large amounts. Then a poor widow came and dropped in two pennies.[9] He called his disciples to him and said, "I assure you, this poor widow has given more than all the others have given. For they gave a tiny part of their surplus, but she, poor as she is, has given everything she has."

CHAPTER 13

Jesus Foretells the Future

As Jesus was leaving the Temple that day, one of his disciples said, "Teacher, look at these tremendous buildings! Look at the massive stones in the walls!"

Jesus replied, "These magnificent buildings will be so completely demolished that not one stone will be left on top of another."

Later, Jesus sat on the slopes of the Mount of Olives across the valley from the Temple. Peter, James, John and Andrew came to him privately and asked him, "When will all this take place? And will there be any sign ahead of time to show us when all this will be fulfilled?"

Jesus replied, "Don't let anyone mislead you, because many will come in my name, claiming to be the Messiah.[1] They will lead many astray. And wars will break out near and far, but don't panic. Yes, these things must come, but the end won't follow immediately. Nations and kingdoms will proclaim war against each other, and there will be earthquakes in many parts of the world, and famines. But all this will be only the beginning of the horrors to come. But when these things begin to happen, watch out! You will be handed over to the courts and beaten in the synagogues. You will be accused before governors and kings of being my followers. This will be your opportunity to tell them about me.[2] And the Good News must first be preached to every nation. But when you are arrested and stand trial, don't worry about what to say in your defence. Just say what God tells you to. Then it is not you who will be speaking, but the Holy Spirit.

"Brother will betray brother to death, fathers will betray their own children, and children will rise against their parents and cause them to be killed. And everyone will hate you because of your allegiance to me. But those who endure to the end will be saved.

"The time will come when you will see the sacrilegious object that causes desecration[3] standing where it should not be" — reader, pay attention! "Then those in Judea must flee to the hills. A person outside the house[4] must not go back into the house to pack. A person in the field must not return even to get a coat. How terrible it will be for pregnant women and for mothers nursing their babies in those days. And pray that your flight will not be in winter. For those will be days of greater horror than at any time since God created the world. And it will never happen again. In fact, unless the Lord shortens that time of calamity, the entire human race will be destroyed. But for the sake of his chosen ones he has shortened those days.

"And then if anyone tells you, 'Look, here is the Messiah,' or, 'There he is,' don't pay any attention. For false messiahs and false prophets will rise up and perform miraculous signs and wonders so as to deceive, if possible, even God's chosen ones. Watch out! I have warned you!

"At that time, after those horrible days end,
the sun will be darkened,
the moon will not give light,
the stars will fall from the sky,
and the powers of heaven will be shaken.[5]

Then everyone will see the Son of Man arrive on the clouds with great power and glory.[6] And he will send forth his angels to gather together his chosen ones from all over the world — from the farthest ends of the earth and heaven.

"Now, learn a lesson from the fig tree. When its buds become tender and its leaves begin to sprout, you know without being told that summer is near. Just so, when you see the events I've described beginning to happen, you can be sure that his return is very near, right at the door. I assure you, this generation[7] will not pass from the scene until all these events have taken place. Heaven and earth will disappear, but my words will remain for ever.

"However, no one knows the day or hour when these things will happen, not even the angels in heaven or the Son himself. Only the Father knows. And since you don't know when they will happen, stay alert and keep watch.[8]

"The coming of the Son of Man can be compared with that of a man who left home to go on a trip. He gave each of his employees instructions about the work they were to do, and he told the gatekeeper to watch for his return. So keep a sharp lookout! For you do not know when the home-owner will return — at evening, midnight, early dawn or late daybreak. Don't let him find you sleeping when he arrives without warning. What I say to you I say to everyone: Watch for his return!"

CHAPTER 14

Jesus Anointed at Bethany

It was now two days before the Passover celebration and the Festival of Unleavened Bread. The leading priests and the teachers of religious law were still looking for an opportunity to capture Jesus secretly and put him to death. "But not during the Passover," they agreed, "or there will be a riot."

Meanwhile, Jesus was in Bethany at the home of Simon, a man who had leprosy. During supper, a woman came in with a beautiful jar of expensive perfume.[1] She broke the seal and poured the perfume over his head. Some of those at the table were indignant. "Why was this expensive perfume wasted?" they asked. "She could have sold it for a small fortune[2] and given the money to the poor!" And they scolded her harshly.

But Jesus replied, "Leave her alone. Why berate her for doing such a good thing to me? You will always have the poor among you, and you can help them whenever you want to. But I will not be here with you much longer. She has done what she could and has anointed my body for burial ahead of time. I assure you, wherever the Good News is preached throughout the world, this woman's deed will be talked about in her memory."

Judas Agrees to Betray Jesus

Then Judas Iscariot, one of the twelve disciples, went to the leading priests to arrange to betray Jesus to them. The leading priests were delighted when they heard why he had come, and they promised him a reward. So he began looking for the right time and place to betray Jesus.

The Last Supper

On the first day of the Festival of Unleavened Bread (the day the Passover lambs were sacrificed), Jesus' disciples asked him, "Where do you want us to go to prepare the Passover supper?"

So Jesus sent two of them into Jerusalem to make the arrangements. "As you go into the city," he told them, "a man carrying a pitcher of water will meet you. Follow him. At the house he enters, say to the owner, 'The Teacher asks: Where is the guest room where I can eat the Passover meal with my disciples?' He will take you upstairs to a large room that is already set up. That is the place; go ahead and prepare our supper there." So the two disciples went on ahead into the city and found everything just as Jesus had said, and they prepared the Passover supper there.

In the evening Jesus arrived with the twelve disciples. As they were sitting around the table eating, Jesus said, "The truth is, one of you will betray me, one of you who is here eating with me."

Greatly distressed, one by one they began to ask him, "I'm not the one, am I?"

He replied, "It is one of you twelve, one who is eating with me now.[3] For I, the Son of Man, must die, as the Scriptures declared long ago. But how terrible it will be for my betrayer. Far better for him if he had never been born!"

As they were eating, Jesus took a loaf of bread and asked God's blessing on it. Then he broke it in pieces and gave it to the disciples, saying, "Take it, for this is my body."

And he took a cup of wine and gave thanks to God for it.

47

He gave it to them, and they all drank from it. And he said to them, "This is my blood, poured out for many, sealing the covenant[4] between God and his people. I solemnly declare that I will not drink wine again until that day when I drink it new in the Kingdom of God." Then they sang a hymn and went out to the Mount of Olives.

Jesus Predicts Peter's Denial

"All of you will desert me," Jesus told them. "For the Scriptures say,

  'God[5] will strike the Shepherd,
  and the sheep will be scattered.'[6]

But after I am raised from the dead, I will go ahead of you to Galilee and meet you there."

Peter said to him, "Even if everyone else deserts you, I never will."

"Peter," Jesus replied, "the truth is, this very night, before the cock crows twice, you will deny me three times."

"No!" Peter insisted. "Not even if I have to die with you! I will never deny you!" And all the others vowed the same.

Jesus Prays in Gethsemane

And they came to an olive grove called Gethsemane, and Jesus said, "Sit here while I go and pray." He took Peter, James and John with him, and he began to be filled with horror and deep distress. He told them, "My soul is crushed with grief to the point of death. Stay here and watch with me."

He went on a little farther and fell face down on the ground. He prayed that, if it were possible, the awful hour awaiting him might pass him by. "Abba,[7] Father," he said, "everything is possible for you. Please take this cup of suffering away from me. Yet I want your will, not mine."

Then he returned and found the disciples asleep. "Simon!" he said to Peter. "Are you asleep? Couldn't you stay awake and watch with me for even one hour? Keep alert and pray. Otherwise temptation will overpower you. For though the spirit is willing enough, the body is weak."

Then Jesus left them again and prayed, repeating his pleadings. Again he returned to them and found them sleeping, for they just couldn't keep their eyes open. And they didn't know what to say.

When he returned to them the third time, he said, "Still sleeping? Still resting?[8] Enough! The time has come. I, the Son of Man, am betrayed into the hands of sinners. Up, let's be going. See, my betrayer is here!"

Jesus Is Betrayed and Arrested

And immediately, as he said this, Judas, one of the twelve disciples, arrived with a mob that was armed with swords and clubs. They had been sent out by the leading priests, the teachers of religious law, and the other leaders. Judas had given them a pre-arranged signal: "You will know which one to arrest when I go over and give him the kiss of greeting. Then you can take him away under guard."

As soon as they arrived, Judas walked up to Jesus. "Teacher!" he exclaimed, and gave him the kiss. Then the others grabbed Jesus and arrested him. But someone pulled out a sword and slashed off an ear of the high priest's servant.

Jesus asked them, "Am I some dangerous criminal, that you come armed with swords and clubs to arrest me? Why didn't you arrest me in the Temple? I was there teaching every day. But these things are happening to fulfil what the Scriptures say about me."

Meanwhile, all his disciples deserted him and ran away. There was a young man following along behind, clothed only in a linen nightshirt. When the mob tried to grab him, they tore off his clothes, but he escaped and ran away naked.

Jesus before the Council

Jesus was led to the high priest's home where the leading priests, other leaders and teachers of religious law had gathered. Meanwhile, Peter followed far behind and then slipped inside the gates of the high priest's courtyard. For a while he sat with the guards, warming himself by the fire.

Inside, the leading priests and the entire high council[9] were trying to find witnesses who would testify against Jesus, so they could put him to death. But their efforts were in vain. Many false witnesses spoke against him, but they contradicted each other. Finally, some men stood up to testify against him with this lie: "We heard him say, 'I will destroy this Temple made with human hands, and in three days I will build another, made without human hands.'" But even then they didn't get their stories straight!

Then the high priest stood up before the others and asked Jesus, "Well, aren't you going to answer these charges? What do you have to say for yourself?" Jesus made no reply. Then the high priest asked him, "Are you the Messiah, the Son of the blessed God?"

Jesus said, "I am, and you will see me, the Son of Man, sitting at God's right hand in the place of power and coming back on the clouds of heaven."[10]

Then the high priest tore his clothing to show his horror

and said, "Why do we need other witnesses? You have all heard his blasphemy. What is your verdict?" And they all condemned him to death.

Then some of them began to spit at him, and they blindfolded him and hit his face with their fists. "Who hit you that time, you prophet?" they jeered. And even the guards were hitting him as they led him away.

Peter Denies Jesus

Meanwhile, Peter was below in the courtyard. One of the servant girls who worked for the high priest noticed Peter warming himself at the fire. She looked at him closely and then said, "You were one of those with Jesus, the Nazarene."

Peter denied it. "I don't know what you're talking about," he said, and he went out into the entryway. Just then, a cock crowed.[11]

The servant girl saw him standing there and began telling the others, "That man is definitely one of that group!" Peter denied it again.

A little later some other bystanders began saying to Peter, "You must be one of that group because you are from Galilee."

Peter said, "I swear by God, I don't know this man you're talking about." And immediately the cock crowed the second time. Suddenly, Jesus' words flashed through Peter's mind: "Before the cock crows twice, you will deny me three times." And he broke down and cried.

CHAPTER 15

Jesus' Trial before Pilate

Very early in the morning the leading priests, other leaders and teachers of religious law — the entire high council[1] — met to discuss their next step. They bound Jesus and took him to Pilate, the Roman governor.

Pilate asked Jesus, "Are you the King of the Jews?"

Jesus replied, "Yes, it is as you say."

Then the leading priests accused him of many crimes, and Pilate asked him, "Aren't you going to say something? What about all these charges against you?" But Jesus said nothing, much to Pilate's surprise.

Now it was the governor's custom to release one prisoner each year at Passover time — anyone the people requested. One of the prisoners at that time was Barabbas, convicted along with others for murder during an insurrection. The mob began to crowd in towards Pilate, asking him to release a prisoner as usual. "Should I give you the King of the Jews?" Pilate asked. (For he realized by now that the leading priests had arrested Jesus out of envy.) But at this point the leading priests stirred up the mob to demand the release of Barabbas instead of Jesus. "But if I release Barabbas," Pilate asked them, "what should I do with this man you call the King of the Jews?"

They shouted back, "Crucify him!"

"Why?" Pilate demanded. "What crime has he committed?"

But the crowd only roared the louder, "Crucify him!"

So Pilate, anxious to please the crowd, released Barabbas to them. He ordered Jesus flogged with a

lead-tipped whip, then turned him over to the Roman
soldiers to crucify him.

The Soldiers Mock Jesus

The soldiers took him into their headquarters[2] and called
out the entire battalion. They dressed him in a purple robe
and made a crown of long, sharp thorns and put it on his
head. Then they saluted, yelling, "Hail! King of the Jews!"
And they beat him on the head with a stick, spat on him
and dropped to their knees in mock worship. When they
were finally tired of mocking him, they took off the purple
robe and put his own clothes on him again. Then they led
him away to be crucified.

The Crucifixion

A man named Simon, who was from Cyrene,[3] was coming
in from the country just then, and they forced him to carry
Jesus' cross. (Simon was the father of Alexander and
Rufus.) And they brought Jesus to a place called Golgotha
(which means Skull Hill). They offered him wine drugged
with myrrh, but he refused it. Then they nailed him to the
cross. They gambled for his clothes, throwing dice[4] to
decide who would get them.

   It was nine o'clock in the morning when the crucifixion
took place. A signboard was fastened to the cross above
Jesus' head, announcing the charge against him. It read:
"The King of the Jews." Two criminals were crucified with
him, their crosses on either side of his.[5] And the people
passing by shouted abuse, shaking their heads in mockery.
"Ha! Look at you now!" they yelled at him. "You can
destroy the Temple and rebuild it in three days, can you?
Well then, save yourself and come down from the cross!"

The leading priests and teachers of religious law also mocked Jesus. "He saved others," they scoffed, "but he can't save himself! Let this Messiah, this king of Israel, come down from the cross so we can see it and believe him!" Even the two criminals who were being crucified with Jesus ridiculed him.

The Death of Jesus

At noon, darkness fell across the whole land until three o'clock. Then, at that time Jesus called out with a loud voice, *"Eloi, Eloi, lema sabachthani?"* which means, "My God, my God, why have you forsaken me?"[6]

Some of the bystanders misunderstood and thought he was calling for the prophet Elijah. One of them ran and filled a sponge with sour wine, holding it up to him on a stick so he could drink. "Leave him alone. Let's see whether Elijah will come and take him down!" he said.

Then Jesus uttered another loud cry and breathed his last. And the curtain in the Temple was torn in two, from top to bottom. When the Roman officer who stood facing him saw how he had died, he exclaimed, "Truly, this was the Son of God!"

Some women were there, watching from a distance, including Mary Magdalene, Mary (the mother of James the younger and of Joseph[7]) and Salome. They had been followers of Jesus and had cared for him while he was in Galilee. Then they and many other women had come with him to Jerusalem.

The Burial of Jesus

This all happened on Friday, the day of preparation,[8] the day before the Sabbath. As evening approached, an honoured member of the high council, Joseph from Arimathea (who was waiting for the Kingdom of God to come), gathered his courage and went to Pilate to ask for Jesus' body. Pilate couldn't believe that Jesus was already dead, so he called for the Roman military officer in charge and asked him. The officer confirmed the fact, and Pilate told Joseph he could have the body. Joseph bought a long sheet of linen cloth, and taking Jesus' body down from the cross, he wrapped it in the cloth and laid it in a tomb that had been carved out of the rock. Then he rolled a stone in front of the entrance. Mary Magdalene and Mary the mother of Joseph saw where Jesus' body was laid.

CHAPTER 16

The Resurrection

The next evening, when the Sabbath ended, Mary Magdalene and Salome and Mary the mother of James went out and purchased burial spices to put on Jesus' body. Very early on Sunday morning,[1] just at sunrise, they came to the tomb. On the way they were discussing who would roll the stone away from the entrance to the tomb. But when they arrived, they looked up and saw that the stone — a very large one — had already been rolled aside. So they entered the tomb, and there on the right sat a young man clothed in a white robe. The women were startled, but the angel said, "Do not be so surprised. You are looking for Jesus, the Nazarene, who was crucified. He isn't here! He has been raised from the dead! Look, this is where they laid his body. Now go and give this message to his disciples, including Peter: Jesus is going ahead of you to Galilee. You will see him there, just as he told you before he died!" The women fled from the tomb, trembling and bewildered, saying nothing to anyone because they were too frightened to talk.[2]

Shorter Ending of Mark
Then they reported all these instructions briefly to Peter and his companions. Afterwards Jesus himself sent them out from east to west with the sacred and unfailing message of salvation that gives eternal life. Amen.

Longer Ending of Mark
It was early on Sunday morning when Jesus rose from the dead, and the first person who saw him was Mary Magdalene, the woman from whom he had cast out seven demons. She went and found the disciples, who were grieving and weeping. But when she told them that Jesus was alive and she had seen him, they didn't believe her.

Afterwards he appeared to two who were walking from Jerusalem into the country, but they didn't recognize him at first because he had changed his appearance. When they realized who he was, they rushed back to tell the others, but no one believed them.

Still later he appeared to the eleven disciples as they were eating together. He rebuked them for their unbelief — their stubborn refusal to believe those who had seen him after he had risen.

And then he told them, "Go into all the world and preach the Good News to everyone, everywhere. Anyone who believes and is baptized will be saved. But anyone who refuses to believe will be condemned. These signs will accompany those who believe: They will cast out demons in my name, and they will speak new languages.[3] They will be able to handle snakes with safety, and if they drink anything poisonous, it won't hurt them. They will be able to place their hands on the sick and heal them."

When the Lord Jesus had finished talking with them, he was taken up into heaven and sat down in the place of honour at God's right hand. And the disciples went everywhere and preached, and the Lord worked with them, confirming what they said by many miraculous signs.

FOOTNOTES

CHAPTER 1
1 Some manuscripts do not include *the Son of God*.
2 Mal 3:1.
3 Isa 40:3.
4 Greek *preaching a baptism of repentance for the forgiveness of sins*.
5 Greek *to stoop down and untie his sandals*.
6 Or *in*; also in 1:8b.
7 *Simon* is called *Peter* in 3:16 and thereafter.
8 Some manuscripts read *Moved with anger*.

CHAPTER 2
1 Greek *the scribes of the Pharisees*.
2 Greek *with tax collectors and sinners*.

CHAPTER 3
1 Some manuscripts do not include *calling them apostles*.
2 Greek *whom he named Boanerges, which means Sons of Thunder*.
3 Greek *the Cananean*.
4 Greek *Beelzeboul*.
5 Or *One cannot rob Satan's kingdom without first tying him up. Only then can his demons be cast out.*
6 Some manuscripts do not include *and sisters*.

CHAPTER 4

1 Isa 6:9-10.

CHAPTER 5

1 Some manuscripts read *Gadarenes;* others read *Gergesenes.* See Matt 8:28; Luke 8:26.
2 Greek *Decapolis.*
3 Greek text uses Aramaic "*Talitha cumi*" and then translates it as "Get up, little girl."

CHAPTER 6

1 Greek *Joses;* see Matt 13:55.
2 Some manuscripts read *He was saying.*
3 Some manuscripts read *the daughter of Herodias herself.*
4 Greek *200 denarii.* A denarius was the equivalent of a full day's wage.
5 Greek *About the fourth watch of the night.*

CHAPTER 7

1 Greek *washed with the fist.*
2 Some Greek manuscripts add *and dining couches.*
3 Isa 29:13.
4 Exod 20:12; 21:17; Lev 20:9; Deut 5:16.
5 Greek '*What I could have given to you is Corban*' (that is, a gift).
6 Some manuscripts add verse 16, *Anyone who is willing to hear should listen and understand.*
7 Some manuscripts add *and Sidon.*
8 Greek *Let the children eat first.*
9 Greek *Decapolis.*
10 Greek text uses Aramaic "*Ephphatha*" and then translates it as "Be opened."

CHAPTER 8

1 Jer 5:21.
2 Or *and began to correct him.*
3 Or *your life;* also in 8:37.

CHAPTER 9

1 Or *shelters;* Greek reads *tabernacles.*
2 Or *become weak.*
3 Some manuscripts add *and fasting.*

4 Greek *enter life;* also in 9:45.
5 Some manuscripts add verse 44 (which is identical with 9:48).
6 Some manuscripts add verse 46 (which is identical with 9:48).
7 Isa 66:24.
8 Greek *salted with fire.* Some manuscripts add *and every sacrifice will be salted with salt.*

CHAPTER 10
1 Deut 24:1.
2 Gen 1:27; 5:2.
3 Some manuscripts do not include *and is joined to his wife.*
4 Gen 2:24.
5 Exod 20:12-16; Deut 5:16-20.
6 Some manuscripts add *for those who trust in riches.*
7 Greek *But many who are first will be last; and the last, first.*
8 Or *on the way.*

CHAPTER 11
1 Greek *Hosanna,* an exclamation of praise that literally means
   "save now";
   also in 11:10.
2 Ps 118:25-26; 148:1.
3 Isa 56:7; Jer 7:11.
4 Greek *they;* some manuscripts read *he.*
5 Some manuscripts add verse 26, *But if you do not forgive, neither will your Father who is in heaven forgive your sins.*
6 Or *By whose authority do you do these things?*

CHAPTER 12
1 Ps 118:22-23.
2 Greek *a denarius.*
3 Deut 25:5-6.
4 Greek *in the story of the bush? God said to him.*
5 Exod 3:6.
6 Deut 6:4-5.
7 Lev 19:18.
8 Ps 110:1.
9 Greek *2 lepta, which is a kodrantes.*

CHAPTER 13
1 Greek *name, saying, 'I am.'*
2 Or *This will be your testimony against them.*
3 Greek *the abomination of desolation.* See Dan 9:27; 11:31; 12:11.
4 Greek *on the roof.*
5 See Isa 13:10; 34:4; Joel 2:10.
6 See Dan 7:13.
7 Or *this age,* or *this nation.*
8 Some manuscripts add *and pray.*

CHAPTER 14
1 Greek *an alabaster jar of expensive ointment, pure nard.*
2 Greek *300 denarii.* A denarius was the equivalent of a full day's wage.
3 Or *one who is dipping bread into the bowl with me.*
4 Some manuscripts read *the new covenant.*
5 Greek *I.*
6 Zech 13:7.
7 *Abba* is an Aramaic term for "father".
8 Or *Sleep on, take your rest.*
9 Greek *the Sanhedrin.*
10 See Ps 110:1; Dan 7:13.
11 Some manuscripts do not include *Just then, a cock crowed.*

CHAPTER 15
1 Greek *the Sanhedrin;* also in 15:43.
2 Greek *the courtyard, which is the praetorium.*
3 *Cyrene* was a city in northern Africa.
4 Greek *casting lots.* See Ps 22:18.
5 Some manuscripts add verse 28, *And the Scripture was fulfilled that said, "He was counted among those who were rebels."* See Isa 53:12.
6 Ps 22:1.
7 Greek *Joses;* also in 15:47. See Matt 27:56.
8 Greek *on the day of preparation.*

CHAPTER 16
1 Greek *on the first day of the week;* also in 16:9.
2 The most reliable early manuscripts conclude the Gospel of Mark at verse 8. Other manuscripts include various endings to the Gospel. Two of the more noteworthy endings are printed here.
3 Or *new tongues;* some manuscripts omit *new.*

Please complete in block capitals or clear print. Thank you

I would like to know more about Jesus and how he can help in my life.

Title: _____

Name: _____

Address: _____

Town: _____

County: _____ Postcode: _____

Please circle your age

-16   16-20   21-40   41-60   60+

Please tick the following as applicable
❏ Would you like some free literature but no personal contact?

   Would you like a local Christian to contact you by...
❏ Letter   ❏ Visit   ❏ Phone
                      (Tel No: _____)

Would you like to know more about a particular church or churches? If, so please state which. If you wish, you may also give some brief details about yourself
(e.g. whether you have any religious background or church connection).

_____

_____

_____

_____

_____

Signature: _____

If you want to know more about the change that Jesus can make in your life, you might like to send off the form on the next page. The Christian Enquiry Agency (CEA) will put you in touch with Christians in your area - although no one will call or phone you unless you specifically ask them to. The CEA is supported by all the major churches.

Please cut this form out and put it in an envelope addressed to: (no stamp required if posted in the United Kingdom)

Christian Enquiry Agency (STL)
FREEPOST
SE 5940
London
SE1 7YX